VOLUME 4

SING WITH THE CHOIR

CD INCLUDED

The 1950s

CONTENTS

ISBN 978-1-4234-3740-6

T0056157

HAL•LEONARD® CORPORATION

7777 W. BLUEMOUND RD. P.O. BOX 13819 MILWAUKEE, WI 53213

Visit Hal Leonard Online at
www.halleonard.com

At the Hop

**Arranged by
ED LOJESKI**

Words and Music by ARTHUR SINGER,
JOHN MADARA and DAVID WHITE

4

Ah,＿＿＿＿＿＿＿＿＿＿＿ Let's go to the hop! *(Let's go!)*

Ah,＿＿＿＿＿＿＿＿＿＿＿

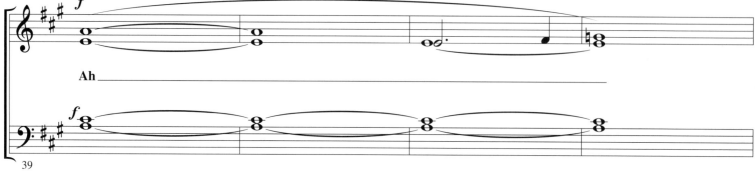

Ah＿＿＿＿＿＿＿＿＿＿＿＿＿＿＿＿＿＿＿＿＿

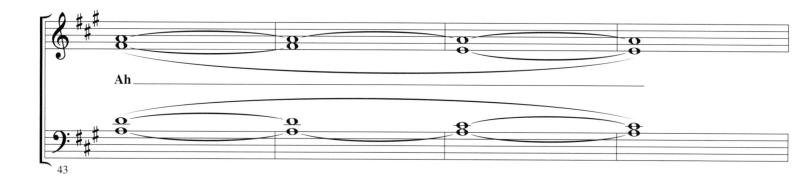

Ah＿＿＿＿＿＿＿＿＿＿＿＿＿＿＿＿＿＿＿＿＿＿＿

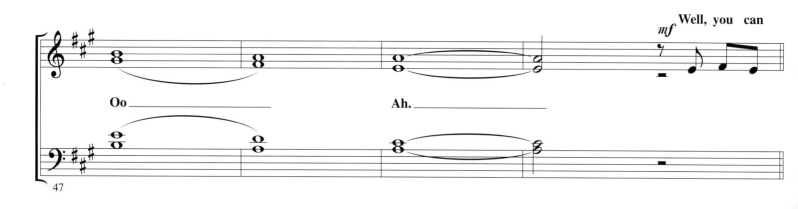

Well, you can

Oo＿＿＿＿＿＿＿＿＿＿   Ah.＿＿＿＿＿＿＿

swing it, you can groove it, you can real - ly start to move it, at the hop.

Hop, hop, hop, hop.   Hop, hop, hop, hop.

Let's go to the hop! Ah,

Let's go to the hop! Oh, ba - by,

Let's go to the hop!

ff Ah,

ff Ah,

Ah,

ff Ah,

Ah,

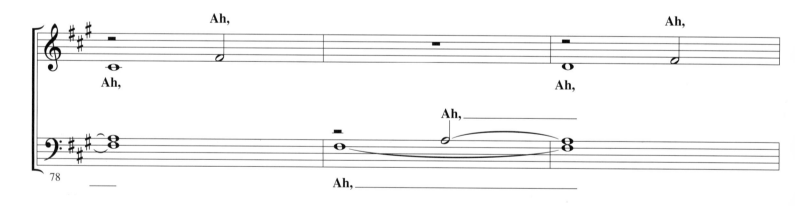

Ah,

Ah,

Ah,

Ah,

Ah,

Ah,

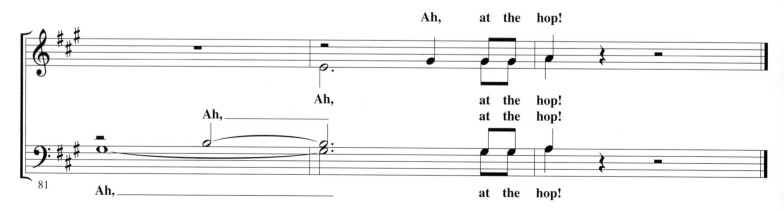

Ah, at the hop!

Ah, at the hop!

Ah, at the hop!

Ah,

Ah, at the hop!

The Great Pretender

Arranged by
ROGER EMERSON

Words and Music by
BUCK RAM

8

Kansas City

Arranged by
MARK BRYMER

Words and Music by **JERRY LEIBER**
and **MIKE STOLLER**

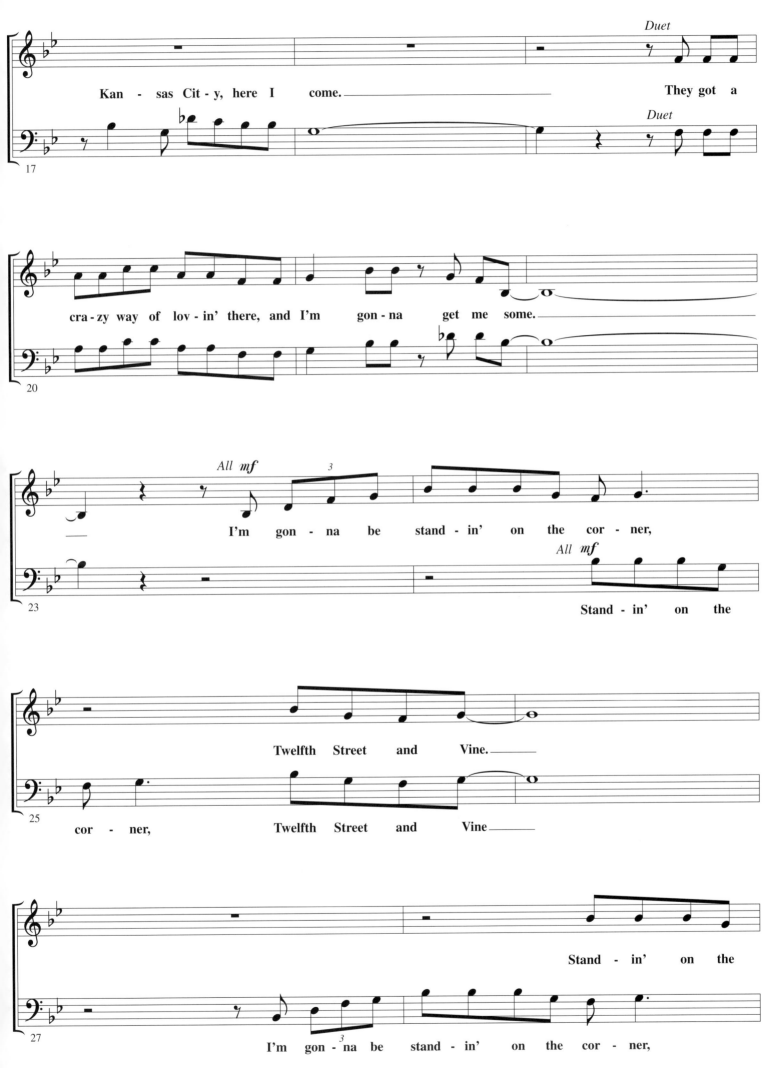

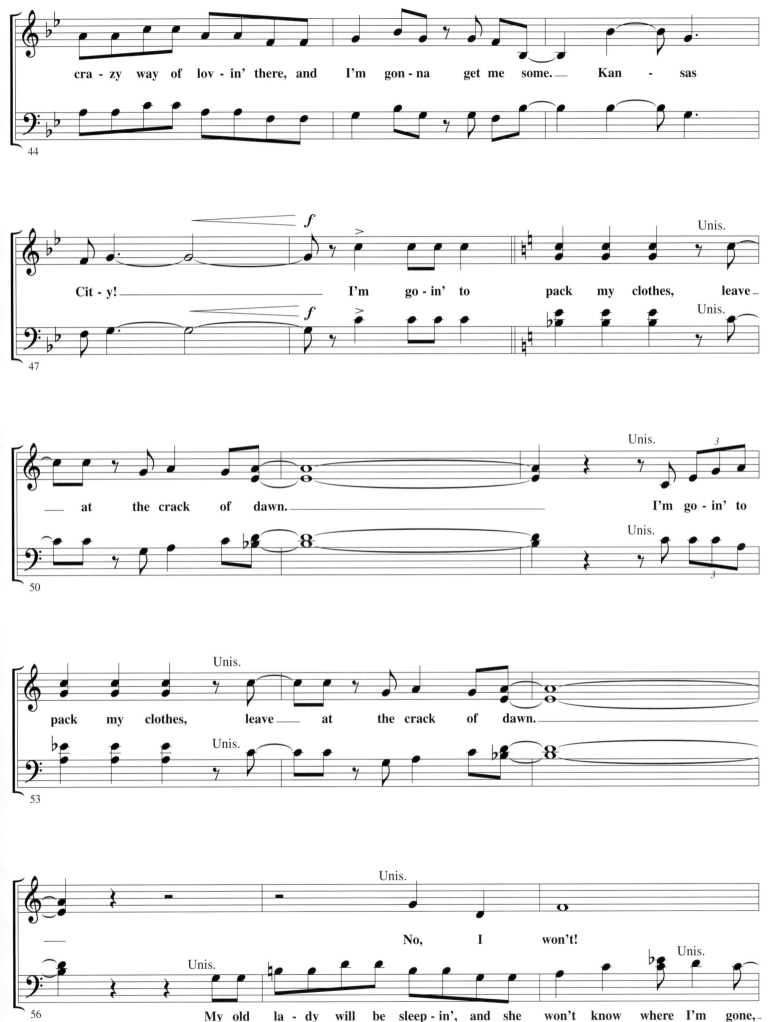

18

I'm gon - na get me some.

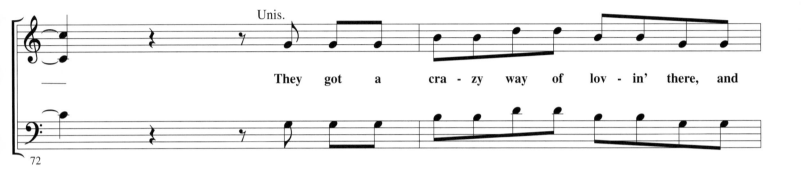

70

Unis.

They got a cra - zy way of lov - in' there, and

72

ff

I'm gon - na get me some.

ff

74

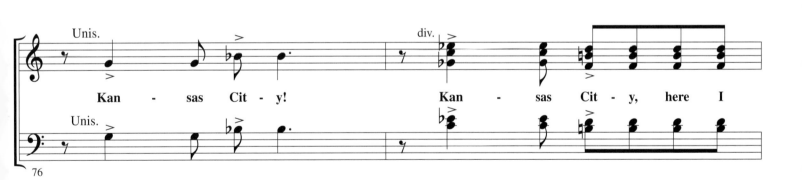

Unis.

Kan - sas Cit - y! Kan - sas Cit - y, here I

Unis.

76

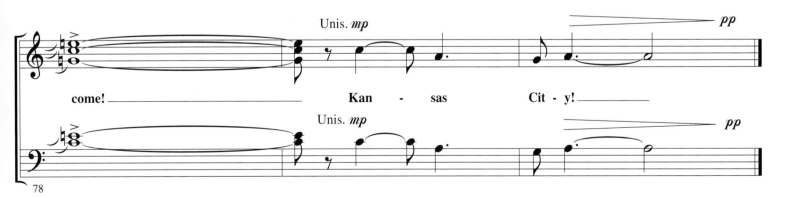

Unis. *mp* *pp*

come! Kan - sas Cit - y!

Unis. *mp* *pp*

78

La Bamba

Arranged by
MARK BRYMER

By RITCHIE VALENS

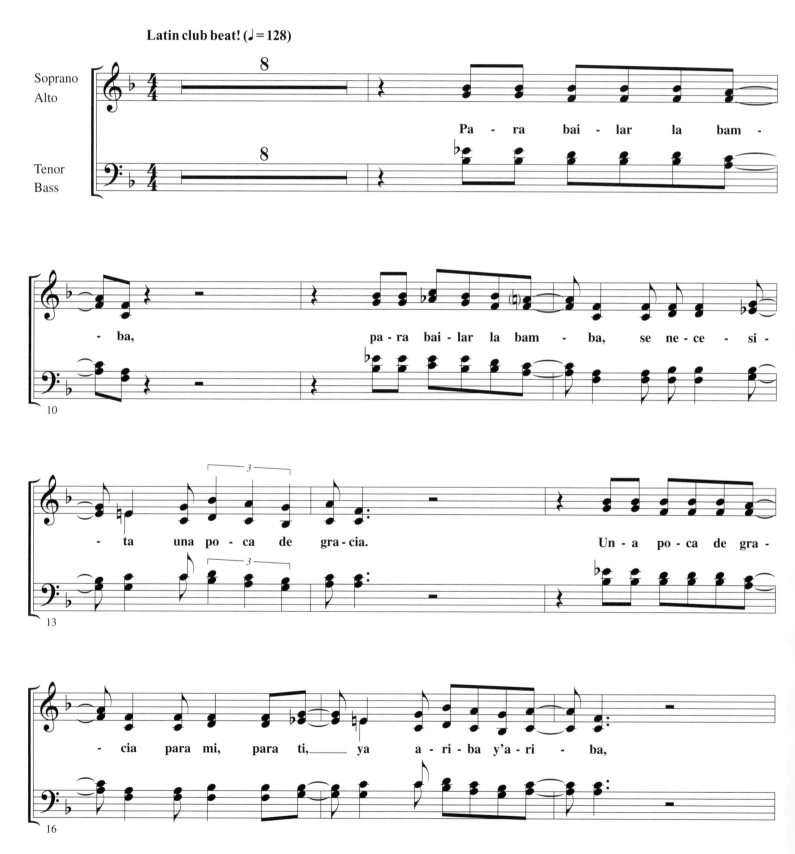

y'a - ri - ba, y'a - ri - ba por ti se - ré____ por ti se - ré____

____ por ti se - ré. Yo no soy mar - i - ne - ro,

yo no soy mar - i - ne - ro, soy cap - i - tan,____ soy cap - i - tan,

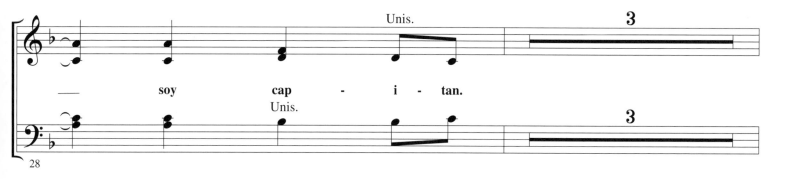

Unis.

____ soy cap - i - tan.
Unis.

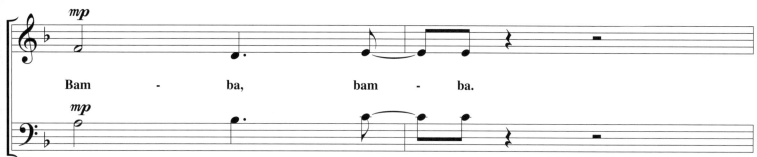

Bam - ba, bam - ba.

Bam - ba, bam - ba. Bam - ba, bam -

- ba. Bam - ba, bam - ba.

Bam - ba,___ bam - ba. Bam - ba, bam -

- ba.___

Pa - ra bai - lar la bam -

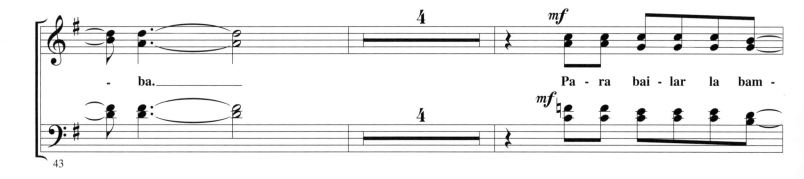

- ba, para bai - lar la bam -

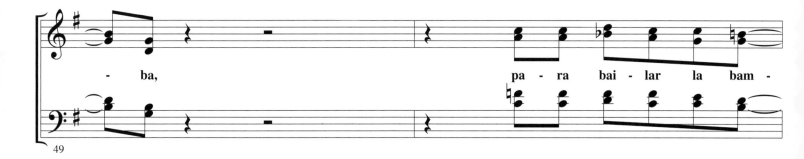

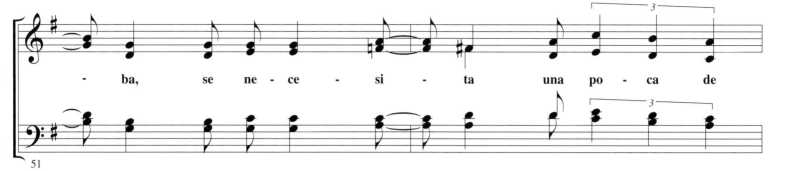

ba, se ne - ce - si - ta una po - ca de

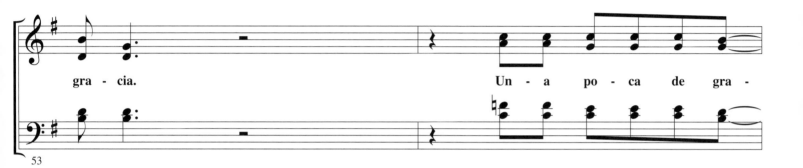

gra - cia. Un - a po - ca de gra -

- cia para mi, para ti,_____ ya a - ri - ba y'a - ri - ba,

y'a - ri - ba, y'a - ri - ba por ti se - ré_____ por ti se - ré_____

_____ por ti se - ré Yo no soy mar - i - ne - ro,

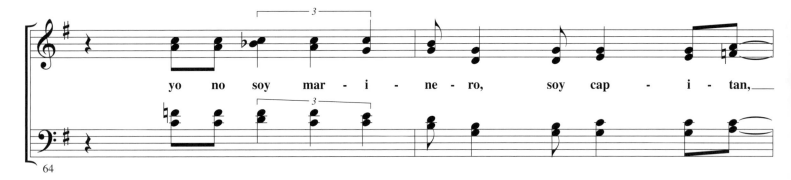

yo no soy mar - i - ne - ro, soy cap - i - tan,___

64

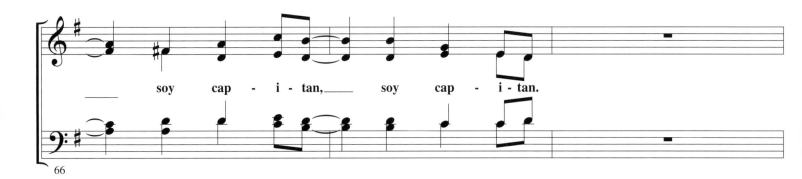

___ soy cap - i - tan,___ soy cap - i - tan.

66

Bam - ba, bam - ba. Bam - ba,___ bam -

69

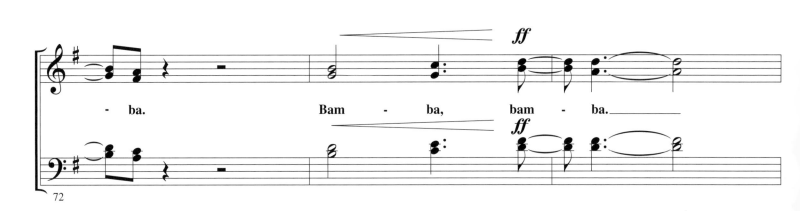

- ba. Bam - ba, bam - ba.___

72

La bam - ba!___

75

Love Me Tender

Arranged by
ROGER EMERSON

Words and Music by ELVIS PRESLEY
and VERA MATSON

My Prayer

Arranged by
ED LOJESKI

Music by GEORGES BOULANGER
Lyric and Musical Adaptation by JIMMY KENNEDY

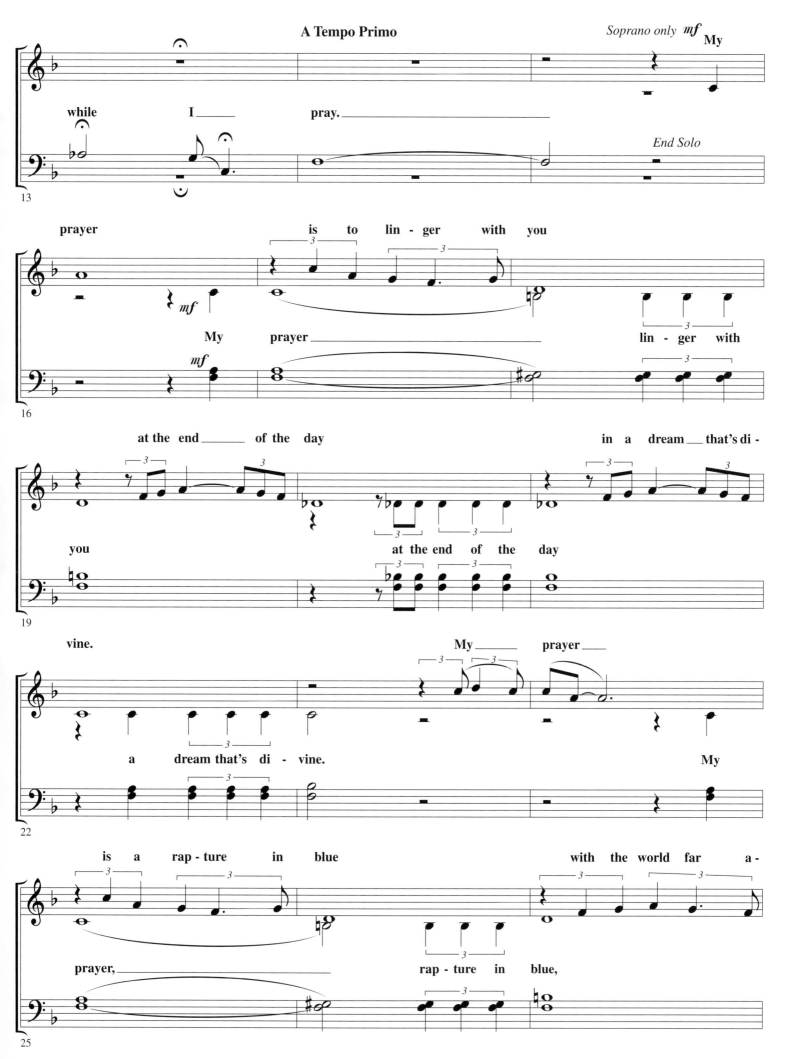

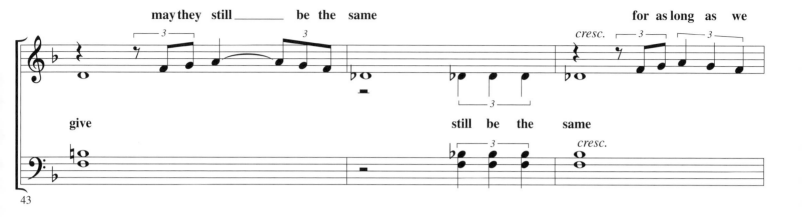

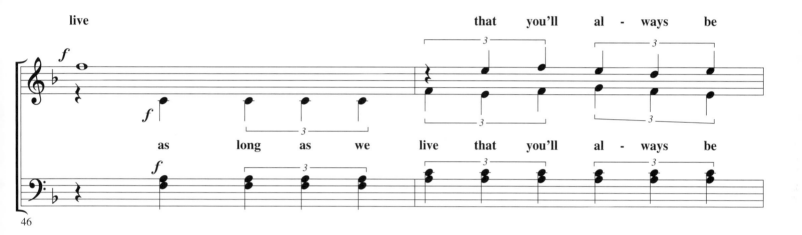

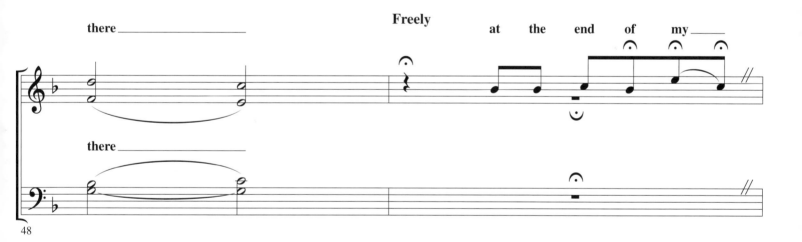

Rock Around the Clock

Arranged by
ROGER EMERSON

Words and Music by MAX C. FREEDMAN
and JIMMY DeKNIGHT

Unchained Melody

Arranged by
MARK BRYMER

Lyric by HY ZARET
Music by ALEX NORTH

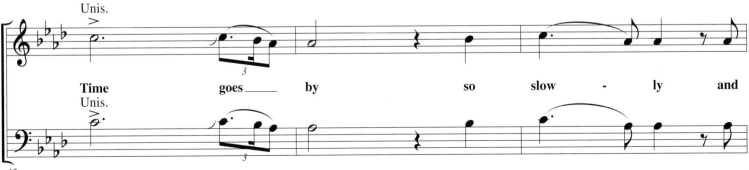

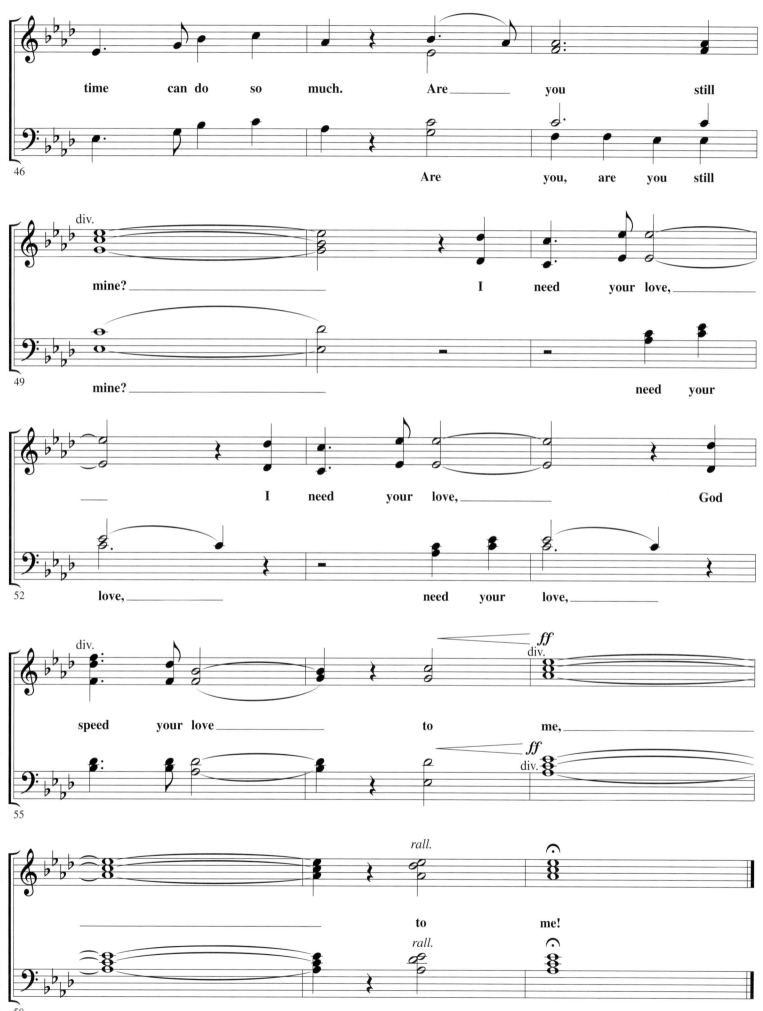

SING WITH THE CHOIR

CD INCLUDED

These GREAT COLLECTIONS let singers
BECOME PART OF A FULL CHOIR and sing along
with some of the most-loved songs of all time.
Each book includes SATB parts (arrangements are enlarged from octavo-size to 9" x 12")
and the accompanying CD features full, professionally recorded performances.

Now you just need to turn on the CD, open the book, pick your part, and
SING ALONG WITH THE CHOIR!

1. ANDREW LLOYD WEBBER

Any Dream Will Do • As If We Never Said Good-bye • Don't Cry for Me Argentina • Love Changes Everything • Memory • The Music of the Night • Pie Jesu • Whistle down the Wind.

00333001 Book/CD Pack................................ $14.95

2. BROADWAY

Bring Him Home • Cabaret • For Good • Luck Be a Lady • Seasons of Love • There's No Business like Show Business • Where Is Love? • You'll Never Walk Alone.

00333002 Book/CD Pack................................ $14.95

3. STANDARDS

Cheek to Cheek • Georgia on My Mind • I Left My Heart in San Francisco • I'm Beginning to See the Light • Moon River • On the Sunny Side of the Street • Skylark • When I Fall in Love.

00333003 Book/CD Pack................................ $14.95

4. THE 1950S

At the Hop • The Great Pretender • Kansas City • La Bamba • Love Me Tender • My Prayer • Rock Around the Clock • Unchained Melody.

00333004 Book/CD Pack................................ $14.95

5. THE 1960S

All You Need is Love • Can't Help Falling in Love • Dancing in the Street • Good Vibrations • I Heard It Through the Grapevine • I'm a Believer • Under the Boardwalk • What a Wonderful World.

00333005 Book/CD Pack................................ $14.95

6. THE 1970S

Ain't No Mountain High Enough • Bohemian Rhapsody • I'll Be There • Imagine • Let It Be • Night Fever • Yesterday Once More • You Are the Sunshine of My Life.

00333006 Book/CD Pack................................ $14.95

7. DISNEY FAVORITES

The Bare Necessities • Be Our Guest • Circle of Life • Cruella De Vil • Friend like Me • Hakuna Matata • Joyful, Joyful • Under the Sea.

00333007 Book/CD Pack................................ $14.95

8. DISNEY HITS

Beauty and the Beast • Breaking Free • Can You Feel the Love Tonight • Candle on the Water • Colors of the Wind • A Whole New World (Aladdin's Theme) • You'll Be in My Heart • You've Got a Friend in Me.

00333008 Book/CD Pack................................ $14.95

9. LES MISÉRABLES

At the End of the Day • Bring Him Home • Castle on a Cloud • Do You Hear the People Sing? • Finale • I Dreamed a Dream • On My Own • One Day More.

00333009 Book/CD Pack................................ $14.95

10. CHRISTMAS FAVORITES

Frosty the Snow Man • The Holiday Season • (There's No Place Like) Home for the Holidays • Little Saint Nick • Merry Christmas, Darling • Santa Claus Is Comin' to Town • Silver Bells • White Christmas.

00333011 Book/CD Pack................................ $14.95

11. CHRISTMAS TIME IS HERE

Blue Christmas • Christmas Time is Here • Feliz Navidad • Happy Xmas (War Is Over) • I'll Be Home for Christmas • Let It Snow! Let It Snow! Let It Snow! • We Need a Little Christmas • Wonderful Christmastime.

00333012 Book/CD Pack................................ $14.95

FOR MORE INFORMATION, SEE YOUR LOCAL MUSIC DEALER,
OR WRITE TO:

HAL•LEONARD®
CORPORATION
7777 W. BLUEMOUND RD. P.O. BOX 13819 MILWAUKEE, WI 53213

Prices, contents, and availability
subject to change without notice.

0508